Dedicated to anyone who has dreamed of running away to sea and starting a new life.

All illustrations and copy are the original and copyrighted work of Quinn Rilley.
First published in 2024

Ching Shih

Many tried to stop them in their tracks.
And hang them for their vile acts.
But some escaped with piles of treasure.
Wealth and fame you couldn't measure.

There are those we remember today.
And their legacy is here to stay.
There's Long John Silver and Black Beard.
Fearsome, bold and highly revered.
Yet there's a buccaneer who didn't enjoy such fame.
Ching Shih was a daring, young dame.

She took on navies from around the world.
Bloody battles soon unfurled.
But Ching Shih would always win.
Leaving her foe in a bit of a spin.

Her story begins aboard a boat.
Where little happened of note.
She would travel from town to city.
To find a port both rough and gritty.

It was here she became a pirate's wife,
which lead her to this notorious life.
She fell in love with a captain who sailed the sea.
He offered her a life both exciting and free.

The pair sailed the seven seas together.
They believed their happiness would last forever.
But Ching Shih was struck down by strife.
Her husband had suddenly lost his life.

She took on the captain's role.
With 80,000 men to control.
Never had there been such a fleet.
Ching Shih, would be hard to defeat.

Aboard her ships were a strict set of laws.
A set of rules to further her cause.

She would steal from every ship she saw,
leaving her enemies in awe.
Many countries grew tired of her stealing their wealth.
She always got their gold using cunning and stealth.
So they sent armoured ships worldwide,
with highly skilled sailors astride.

But Ching Shih was undefeated.
Regardless of who competed.

Eventually she was given a difficult decision.
A choice that could cause some division.
She was asked to retire from her life of piracy.
For a life of quiet privacy.
She'd get to keep all her treasure.
And enjoy a life of leisure.
Ching Shih quickly agreed.
And had a new life to lead.

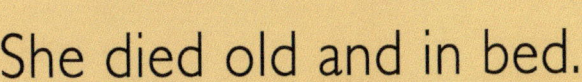

She died old and in bed.
With many memories in her head.
She'd sailed the seven seas.
And did whatever she pleased.

Let's remember Ching Shih; the pirate queen.
The most fearsome the world has ever seen.
She deserves a spot in the pirate hall-of-fame.
Because of her, the seas were never the same.

The End

About Hidden Heroes of Herstory

Have you ever thumbed through a history book and wondered "Why are all these trailblazers mostly men?"

Well, fear not. There is a whole part of history hidden from those dull books. Women from all over the world, have made real leaps forward for humanity.

Hidden Heroes of Herstory aims to tell their stories and bring to life these women, who are often forgotten. We use rhymes and bright images to help tell their stories, so the next generation can remember these heroes and their names will never be forgotten again.

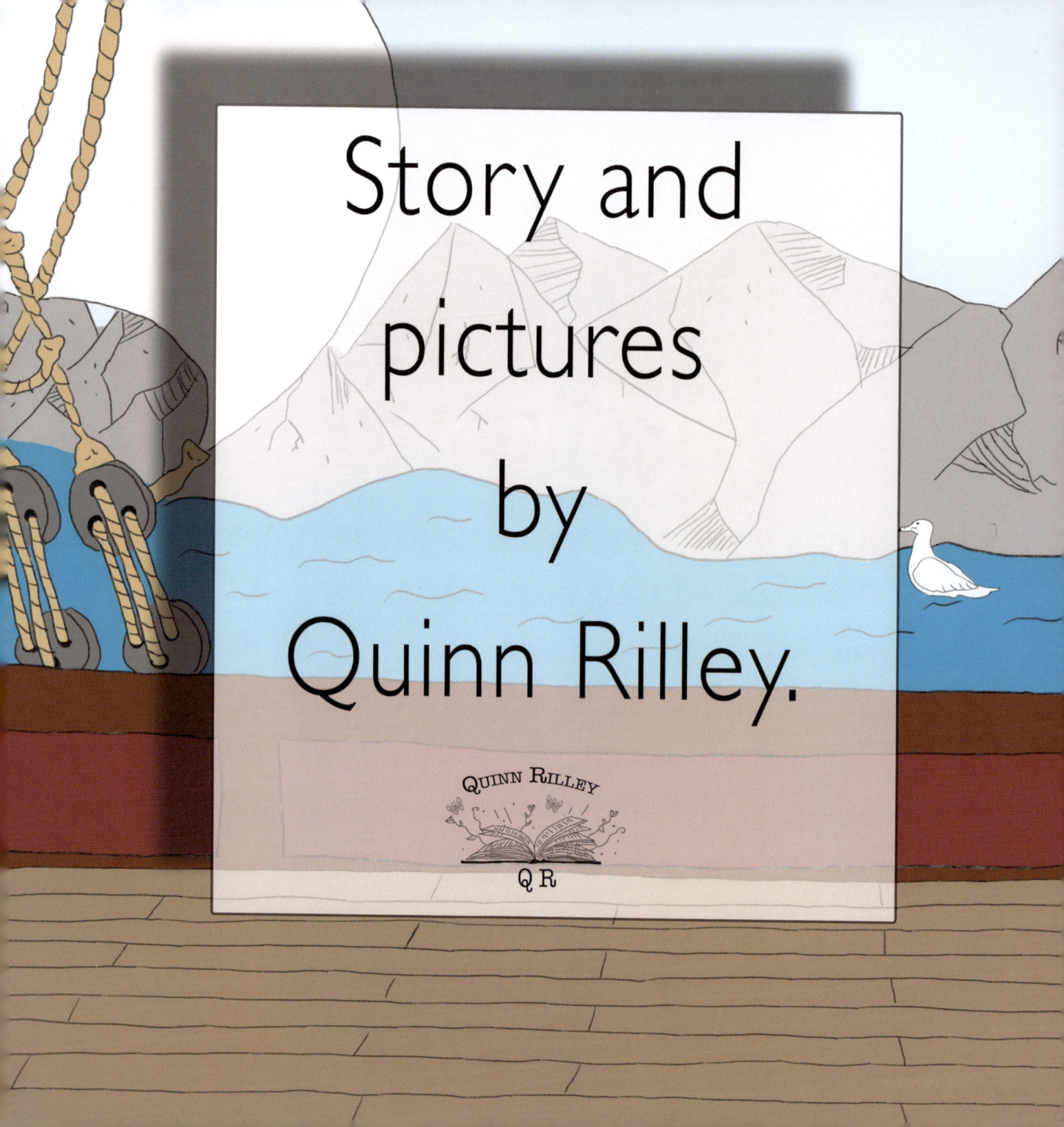

Story and pictures by Quinn Rilley.

Who is this Quinn Rilley anyway?

Quinn Rilley once sat down to do her taxes. Instead her mind wandered and she started to ponder life's most important questions, like 'do penguins have knees?'

To answer this question she went out into the world and befriended a rogue penguin. Who turned out to be a disgruntled, smartly dressed waiter named Dave, and he definitely has knees.

Printed in Great Britain
by Amazon